Hobbo is a grumpy old soul, born and dragged up on a council estate in the foothills of Bradford, West Yorkshire. He has been a police officer in Yorkshire, a dog groomer in France and a bus driver for people with special needs in Lancashire. He began writing humorous poetry as a child and rekindled that childhood passion during the recent spate of pandemic lockdowns.

The author has children in England and Australia, and currently lives in the U.K with his dog, Dauphy, and other members of his family. Hobbo speaks several languages fluently including French, Yorkshire and Lancastrian.

To my best pal Dauphy, without whom this book would not have been possible and my gran for her unfailing encouragement. I still miss you after all these years.

Hobbo

HOBBO ON LIFE

AUSTIN MACAULEY PUBLISHERS™
LONDON • CAMBRIDGE • NEW YORK • SHARJAH

Copyright © Hobbo 2023

The right of Hobbo to be identified as author of this work has been asserted by the author in accordance with sections 77 and 78 of the Copyright, Designs and Patents Act 1988.

All rights reserved. No part of this publication may be reproduced, stored in a retrieval system, or transmitted in any form or by any means, electronic, mechanical, photocopying, recording, or otherwise, without the prior permission of the publishers.

Any person who commits any unauthorised act in relation to this publication may be liable to criminal prosecution and civil claims for damages.

A CIP catalogue record for this title is available from the British Library.

ISBN 9781398470767 (Paperback)
ISBN 9781398470781 (ePub e-book)
ISBN 9781398470774 (Audiobook)

www.austinmacauley.com

First Published 2023
Austin Macauley Publishers Ltd®
1 Canada Square
Canary Wharf
London
E14 5AA

Dot for her patience. Mother Warton for her understated humour and Austin Macauley Publishers for getting me over the line.

Table of Contents

No Rehearsal	17
This Is Your Life	18
The Shopping Trolleys	19
Tempus Fugit	21
The Yorkshire C-Bomb	22
Reason for Everything	23
Just Do It!	24
The Detective	25
Power of the Pen	26
Coincidence or Consequence?	27
Foodbanks	29
True Wisdom	30
If	31
Winning the Lottery	32
You and Me, Me and You	33
An Elegy	34
Friday Nights	35
French Revolution	37
A Yorkshire Rant	38
Chest La Vie	40

The Yorkshire Alphabet	42
Tribute to Wordsworth	43
Listening Skills	44
Things to Do Lists	46
Careful What You Wish For	48
Right Move	49
Excuse Me!	50
Our Cunning Plan	51
Bloodlines	52
Exemption Certificate	53
Amazing Fact	54
Caring Profession	55
You're Having a Laugh! (For the Boys)	56
Dauphy the Dog, Writes a Tanka	57
Classic Car	58
Medical Records	59
Dauphin the Dog's Philosophy	60
We Aim to Please	61
Playing Games	63
Adios Amigo!	64
The Thief	65
The 'E' Plan Diet	66
Monica's Moniker	67
Last Orders Please	68
The Splits	69
Laws of Physics	70
Modern Politics	71

Which Door?	72
Affects 1 in 100	74
Once Upon a Time	76
Hide and Stink	77
Selfless?	78
Boredom	79
Poetry Masterclass (by Dauphin the Dog)	80
Ode to a Bogey	81
Gerry Marsden, How Did You Do It?	82
Time Management	83
The Race	84
Holes	85
Black Clouds	87
The Eve of What?	88
New Covid Rules	89
A Chat with Dauphin the Dog	90
The Meaning of Life	92
Short-Lived Joy	93
Trouble Ahead	94
A Lockdown Ditty	95
The Pharmacy	96
Socks	97
The Mighty Oak	98
Tha'll Need Some PPE (To the tune of Ilkley Moor baht'at)	99
Dream Catcher	101
Christmas 2020	102
The Owl and the Puddy Tat	103

Noah's Muddy Ark	104
Deaf, Me?	105
The Learner	106
Be More Dog! by Dauphin	107
The Generation Gap	108
The Health Check	109
The Restaurant	110
Goosey Goose Gone	111
A Good Night's Sleep	112
The Baffled Blogger	113
Growing Old Gracefully	114
The Art of Biscuit Dunking	115
Perceptions	116
The Big Date	117
Behind the Mask	118
The Daily Paradox	119
Dual Standards	120
Bliss	121
Sisters	122
Happiness	123
Tiers (To Tears, a Song by the Late, Great Ken Dodd)	124
Mrs Hobbo	125
The Church	127
This Is the Baby	128
Autumn	130
My Body	131
Please	132

A Tough Life	134
A Spectacle	135
Hurry Up!	136
The Gift	137
Skin	138
Generosity	139
Votes	140
Friends	141
Things That I Hate (To Favourite Things by Rodgers and Hammerstein)	142
The Wreck	143
Power	144
Hey Diddle Diddle	145
Oh Heck!	146
Planting Babies	147
A Four-Letter Word	148
Loss	150
Bones	151
The Widow	152
Our Pet	153
Trust	154
Lunch	155
Little Old Beer Drinker (To Little Old Wine Drinker, by Dean Martin)	156
A Poem About Anything	157
The Medical	158
Democracy	160

Girl Power	161
Steam	162
Gran's Clock	163
House to Home	164
Grooming	165
Best Holiday Ever	166
My Engine	168
Equality	169
Books	170
Curry	171
Chillin'	172
The Gigolo	173
The Victory	174
Amazing Facts	175
Vandalism	176
Vacation	177
The Flu Jab	178
Question Time	179
Just Eat	180
First Encounter	181
Old Friends	182
Children	183
Tattoos	184
Polly	185
The Canine Poet by Dauphin	186
Predictive Text	187
Choice	188

Pandemic	189
Vanishing Youth	190
Books	191
Compromise	192
Paper	193
I Wandered Lonely	194
Emancipation	195
Owl	196
If Schools	197
Poet's Inheritance	198
Images	199
Springtime	200
Ponder	201
Granddad	202
Politicians	203
Fish and Chips	204
Johnny	205
Dear Diary	206
The Trip	207
The Face	209
Mates	210
Alcohol and Me	211
Eternity	212
Canine Therapy	213
Loyalty	215
The Bookworm	216
Leaves	217

Deafness	218
Cricket	219
A Nod to Mr Lear	220
Yorkshire-Born Rhapsody (To Bohemian Rhapsody by Freddie Mercury)	221
Beefy	224
The Park Bench	225
Old Age Pensioner	226
Shorts	227
Insomnia	228
Covid	229
Black Lives Matter	230

No Rehearsal

The grazing cow, the harvest mouse,
Fear not, the blood red slaughterhouse.
When first a dog looks on your face
She looks for love, not creed or race.

The giant crab or basking skate
They worry not about their fate.
Foresight, it's the curse of man
To know that there's no master plan.

This fear of life, to us unique
Curtails our dreams and makes us weak.
Ephemeral as our beans on toast
Shed those shackles, lay that ghost.

This Is Your Life

Life
may provide
the pen and the paper

But
you
are the one
who writes
the story.

The Shopping Trolleys

Squeaky-wheeled, the shopping cart
Ferries goods around the mart.
In its ever changing hold
Lie lost secrets, never told.

Errant husbands, in a hurry,
Farmer types, who smell of slurry,
Secret Santas, for the office,
Squabbling kids, who fight for toffees.

Fussy sorts, the feely-touchers,
Veggies who avoid the butcher's
Grimy toddlers, babes in nappies,
O.A.Ps, and cheeky chappies.

Lover boys with cheapskate flowers,
Lonely folk, who pass the hours
Chatting with the clientele,
Shopping till that final bell.

Thieves, with no intent to pay,
Drunken louts, who start affrays,
Married couples, taking huff,
Pin-striped suits and working scruffs.

Diets won and diets lost,
Thrifty ones, who count the cost

Of each item, as they pick it,
Mentally arithmetic it.

Coupon warriors, voucher wavers,
Flashy spendthrifts, supersavers,
You've seen us all, know all our tricks,
Now, go and get your damned wheel fixed!

Tempus Fugit

That breath
you have taken,
you will never
breathe again.

The harsh words
you have spoken,
can never
be unsaid.

That memory
you are making,
the teardrop
in your eye
and tomorrow
claims the lot,
everything
a fleeting lie.

Be not afraid
though, little one,
time flies, like this,
for everyone.

The Yorkshire C-Bomb

Tha' cun't use a comb,
Cos thee 'air's a bit sparse,
And tha' cun't marry 'er,
Cos she's gorra fat arse.

Translation
You have no requirement for a comb,
Because you are almost bald,
And you couldn't tie the knot with her,
Because she is rather a large lady!

Reason for Everything

I shave my neck
Most every day,
But, what the heck,
It's here to stay.

In height, my spec
Is fairly tall,
Without a neck,
I'd be quite small.

And goodness me,
If I'd no neck,
I guarantee,
I'd be a wreck.

Just Do It!

You are as unique
as a flake of snow,
though
equally ethereal.

Live now,
fully, quickly,
before
that melt-water.

Not tomorrow.
It may not
arrive.

Today,
do it,
make
that metaphorical
skydive.

The Detective

It's not in the bath,
Not in the sink,
Not in the glass
That I use for a drink.

Not on the flannel,
Or the waste paper basket,
It wouldn't be hard,
If I could but ask it.

Not on the hairbrush,
The cabinet, or
Caught in the towel,
Lost on the floor.

A fingertip search
Of everywhere, no!
Where the hell did
That nail clipping go?

Power of the Pen

A simple signature can;

Acknowledge new life,
or register the end of one.

Declare our undying love,
or send a country to war.

Purchase a property,
or buy us some time.

Make us millionaires,
or turn us bankrupt.

Seal a marriage,
or certify a divorce.

Give the gift of life
or end it all.

Pass me that pen please!

Coincidence or Consequence?

Fat man
Orders a supersized meal.

Coincidence or consequence?

Drug addict
Sleeps on a park bench.

Coincidence or consequence?

Lottery winner
Is desperately lonely.

Coincidence or consequence?

Child abuser
Gets raped in jail.

Coincidence or consequence?

Workaholic
Dies at her desk.
Coincidence or consequence?

Politicians
Are completely distrusted.

Coincidence or consequence?
Non-judgemental people
Live happier, longer lives.

Coincidence or consequence?

Foodbanks

A charitable crutch
For the poor and needy,
Or, an easy touch
For the feckless, greedy?

Mere subsistence,
A basic feed
Or can their existence
Create a need?

Human fuel
Or, a last resort,
The question is cruel,
But, it does need thought.

True Wisdom

A wise man,
knows
everything.

A wise woman,
allows him
to think so.

If

If
the totality of our thoughts
is hatred,
we will perish.

if
the product of our ponderings
is love,
we shall triumph.

Winning the Lottery

I'm more than delighted,
Extremely excited,
Shout it out? No. I could yelp it.
I am over the moon,
And I shouldn't croon,
But, honestly, I cannot help it.

I can now break the rules,
It's like winning the pools,
Buying myself a home brew kit.
I am King of the Hill,
I'm top of the bill,
I really am going to milk it.

Christmas and birthday,
Rolled up into one day,
Luck! I can hardly believe it.
The call said, 'Get there,
We have vaccine to spare,
I've beaten that covid, achieved it!

You and Me, Me and You

You measure success, by your power,
The money you earn by the hour,
Your place at the top of the chart
The people who nod when you fart.

Now, I, am content with my lot
Whereas you (Sir!), quite clearly are not.
I always sleep soundly in bed
But you chase the dreams in your head.

For me, life's a joy and a pleasure,
My family and friends are my treasure
You are constantly searching for more
Never pausing to think, what life's for.

I consider what use I can be
To others, with you, it's all me
For you, a huge house is essential
Though I think it's inconsequential.

Love that we share and we give
Are the tenets by which we should live.
You think that fame is a must,
You forget that we all turn to dust.

When you die, are there people who'll grieve
Or, will they count the money you leave?
Have you spent your time wisely on earth?
It's the value that counts, not the worth.

An Elegy

Here fly the ashes
of Hobbo the Poet.
Life's clock had stopped
before he could slow it.

Friday Nights

Blue lights.
Fist fights.
Fast cars.
Packed bars.
Shrill two-tones
Broken bones.
Thunderstorms.
Uniforms.
Emergency,
To A and E.
Bare flesh teaser.
Pavement pizza.
Takeaway, smells good.
Busted nose, spits blood.
Wrong glance, teenage spat.
What's you looking at?
Vicious looking flick knives.
Liberated housewives.
Atmosphere, electric.
Not again, she's been sick.
Need a leak, take a piss.
All week, work for this.
Feel ill, too much drink.
Bog full, piss in sink.
Cops here, take names.
Stiff them, play games.
Now, feeling ill, I pop a pill.
Final sup,
All fucked up.

Thumping head.
Some guys died.
All flee,
Scot-free
Shit's sake
It's me…

French Revolution

The peasants had started to riot,
Over rumours that caused them disquiet.
There was no cake to scoff
So, Louis the Toff
Was put on a guillotine diet.

A Yorkshire Rant

Tha' mun think that, am med o'brass
Well, shove it up yer Khyber Pass!
Fifty bob, fer chips wi' scraps,
I dun't pay that fer good flat caps!

Tha' thieving sod, tha'll rob me blind,
'all take me stick, 'ave 'alf a mind
To stick it, where the sun don't shine,
Tha' robbin' git, tha' greedy swine.

I'm an O.A.P tha' knows,
I wochit, where me money goes,
So, tha' can keep thee chips, instead '
all mek do wi' some drippin' bread.

Translation
You may think that I have lots of money
Well, you can put that money in your bottom
£2.50 for French fries with trimmings,
It costs me less for decent headgear.

You are a thief who is prepared to scam me
I am inclined to take my walking cane
And put it in a painful place,
You robbing villain, you greedy scoundrel.

*You know I'm an old age pensioner
And I have to be prudent with money*

*So you keep your chips for yourself, whilst I,
Will have some bread spread liberally with pork fat.*

Chest La Vie

Life is
a cornucopia of contrast,
a cruel joke
of juxtapositions.

C'est la vie.

The unimaginable wealth
of royal racehorse owners
and
The life sapping poverty,
of the homeless gambling addict.

C'est la vie.

The limitless optimism
of human ideals
and
the actual reality
of everyday life.

C'est la vie.

The glorious beauty
of planet earth
and
our ugly determination
to destroy it.
C'est la vie.

The corrosive corruption
of absolute power
and
the frustrating impotence
of the powerless.

C'est la vie.

Our futile attempts
at cheating death
and
the inexorable
tramp of time.

C'est la vie.

The carefully crafted images
of the poet's pen
and

the thoughtless hatred
vomited on social media.

C'est la vie!

The Yorkshire Alphabet

A. is food for 'osses.
B. a striped insect that makes 'unny.
C. a big, wavy pond full of fish.
D. a river in Wales.
E. by gum, a fairly meaningless Yorkshire expression.
F. and Jeff, to swear.
G. an expression of delight.
H. the thing a woman will never disclose truthfully.
I. usually come in pairs…used for seeing.
J. a type of bird.
K. a lass's name
L. where I'll likely go after I die.
M. a polite way of interrupting a conversation.
N. a domestic bird, lays eggs for our breakfast.
O. an expression of surprise.
P. done a lot after too much to drink.
Q. an orderly line, peculiar to Brits.
R. a state of existence, as in you R.
S. a whispered affirmation.
T. 'ot beverage, served with biscuits.
U. thee
V. a rude salute.
W. definitely thee.
X. things that 'ens lay.
Y. a toddler's favourite question.
Z. noggin, skull, as in he's off 'is Z.

With thanks to The Two Ronnies and Baldrick from Black Adder for a couple of these definitions!

Tribute to Wordsworth

You wander lonely as a cloud,
Steer clear of all the Covid crowd,
The sight of all those daffodils,
Uplifts your heart, discard those pills.

Listening Skills

I saw Anna in town today.

That dog!

She's had an operation on her foot.

It stinks!

Lisa's had another baby.

It's filthy. Think I'll give it a bath.

They're going abroad this year.

Is the water hot?

That back door needs painting.

Where's the shampoo?

There's some paint in the shed.

Can you use it on dogs?

Do you fancy a holiday?

I'll need a towel.

A little bed and breakfast?

A big one I reckon.

Whereabouts?

On second thoughts.

You choose.

I can't be arsed!

We'll stay at home then.

It doesn't smell that bad.

I'll put the kettle on…

Things to Do Lists

His, during Covid lockdown

1. Shave
2. Shower
3. Feed
4. Watch telly
5. Bed

Hers, during Covid lockdown

1. Clean
2. Cook
3. Wash
4. Shop
5. Vac
6. Dust
7. Iron
8. Drop

His, after Covid lockdown

1. Shave
2. Shower
3. Feed
4. Watch telly
5. Bed

Hers, after Covid lockdown

1. *Buy a season ticket, can they survive the drop?*
2. *Jimmy Choo's size seven, from that designer shop.*
3. *Book foreign holiday, in Italy or Spain.*
4. *Ring up Bob the Builder, to fix that windowpane.*
5. *Meet my friends for coffee, a catch-up, and a chat.*
6. *Renew my gym subscription, got to lose this fat.7.*
7. *Take my mother shopping, but must be M and S.*
8. *Judy could come with us, and pick herself a dress.*
9. *New nail bar in Blackburn, it's doing two for one.*
10. *While I'm being pampered, I'll have my Barnet done.*
11. *Join a local theatre group, for social intercourse.*
12. *Tell my useless husband, I'm filing for divorce.*

Careful What You Wish For

2020
Brexit hogs the headlines
Brexit every day,
Brexit with its deadlines
Please make it go away.

2021
Covid's killed so many
Randomly it slew,
What I'd give for any
Piece of Brexit news.

Right Move

The tortoise and the snail swapped lids,
Hardly so surprising,
Snail needed more room for the kids,
And the tortoise was downsizing.

Excuse Me!

Natural, but unsociable,
are those ill-disciplined
enough to think acceptable,
to let loose their trapped wind!

Our Cunning Plan

No procrastination!
Even if you disagree,
Please get your vaccination
For we have no great 'Plan B'.

Bloodlines

My old man is lying here,
I visit him, but once a year.
Twenty years this blokes been dead
And still he's messing with my head.

Parents nurturing and kind
For me a joke, they screw your mind.
I'm not like them, and God forbid
That I should ever hurt the kids.

Am I any better though?
Ask my sons, for I don't know.

Exemption Certificate

This is to certify that the holder of this certificate is exempt from

Work related exertions;

Manual or retail,
Or office bound with email.

Worry;

Health, wealth, finance
Family or romance.

Possessions;

Financial or property
Crippling abject poverty.

Physical activities;

Everything in real life
Anything but still life.
I further certify that the owner of this certificate is DEAD!

Evan Chewly

Amazing Fact

World's strongest man catches a train.

Caring Profession

A woman with problems, Fallopian
Saw a specialist doc, Ethiopian,
Eighteen kids later
She sued this creator,
For spoiling her lifestyle, Utopian.

You're Having a Laugh!
(For the Boys)

A problem, I had,
I was losing my grip,
Visit the toilet
Then, permanent drip,

You're having a laugh!
Come on, don't deny it.
Urologist grinned,
Just try it, just try it.

When you are finished
Before you re-dress,
Reach behind goolies,
Between your legs, press.

It works every time
Don't know why, don't know how
And who really cares?
I've got dry undies, now!

Dauphy the Dog, Writes a Tanka

They drive their tankas
through the mud, tankity tank,
shooting the enemy.
I'm not scared, I have a bomb
boom boom boom, boom-buddy boom!

Classic Car

The motor belonged to his niece,
But she let him have it, on lease
On lifting the bonnet,
A fourteen line sonnet,
The source of the rhyme, ancient grease.

Medical Records

Today, my virus jab,
Old folks turn, I guess.
"Little prick sir," said the nurse
Politely, I said "yes."

Then I got to wondering
How did she know that?
Do NHS keep records
Of every little fact?

Dauphin the Dog's Philosophy

To train a dog to
sit, you need a dog to train.
To teach a man to fish,
you need a man, a fish
and a flipping good chippy.

We Aim to Please

Now this here's a delicate subject,
Appertaining to only us blokes
As a poet, I cannot ignore it
And it's often the subject of jokes.

I'm talking of bodily functions,
But I'll be as discreet as I can
Womenfolk don't have to read this,
Though I bet, they will sneak a quick scan.

It's all got to do with the diff'rence
What me mam used to call 'dangly bits,
A woman has need of the toilet,
For the whole operation, she sits.

We first find this thing, in our nappies
Such a treasure, for any young boy
Then what does your mum go and tell you,
It's a present, but it's not a toy.

As lads we are given a bucket,
Which we tip upside down, so we reach
We balance on top, and rest on the rim
Missus, watch where you go with that bleach.

Growing up, we are taken to visit
This white shiny thing, the urinal,
The smell when you walk through the door
Can best be described as caninal.

At home, there is nothing, quite like this
Instead, we must target the pan,
It's generally a two handed job
And we aim it, as best as we can.

Now here, lies the crux of the problem,
As we stand there, with hands occupied
Not a care in the world, so we whistle,
Then, the lid on the bog starts to slide.

A dilemma of piddling proportions
How do I, take this matter in hand
Without pissing all over the bathroom
Thereby risking my wife's reprimands.

Quick as a flash, 'ere the lid falls
'Leg lifts, an' I catch it with' knee
But far from an ideal solution
My hands are now covered in wee.

So ladies, when choosing a toilet
Pick one, with a lid what stays put
Don't have them, what drop down while you're streaming, Q.E.D, I think, open and shut.

Playing Games

It's only three letters. Guess it, you're good.

Got it in one! The answer is bud!

Almost correct! 'B' gets you a nod.

So, if I was real close…do you mean bod?

The 'D's' also right, you go wrong in the mid.

This is too easy, you're thinking of bid.

Ever so warm now. Driving you mad?

Nope, I think I've got it. The word must be bad.

'B' something 'D', it's all in your head!

Ah, now I've sussed it. You want me in bed!

Adios Amigo!

Yesterday, Trump was a president
A tweeting, unbeaten sweetheart,
In White House, no longer a resident
Trump again means a windy old fart.

The Thief

Disguised as a friend
who is with us forever,
Old age steals our youth.

The 'E' Plan Diet

This elephant's fat, can't deny it,
Poor Nellie is put on a diet.
She drops two tons in weight,
Though they still fill her plate,
But boil all her food, and don't fry it.

Monica's Moniker

This passion for fashion, in naming our babies,
Alas, will our lass be a Porsche, Mercedes?
Africa, India, Bangalore, Singapore,
Nay, a full football team, if you feel she needs more.
Star, starlight, sun, sunlight, my oh my, even windy
Not you, to make do, with a Barbie or Cindy.
There's no shame in a name, that stands out from the crowd,
Say it loud, say it proud, but for crying out loud,
Remember the name will be with them forever,
You may think it's clever, but don't call her Trevor.

Last Orders Please

Near and *farting*

went the bell
To call last orders.

What's that smell?

The Splits

Should I be going boldly,
Or do I boldly go?
Splitting my infinitive
be a fatal blow.

It's difficult to truly
Write, with realism,
When my native tongue is tied,
Lashed down by dogmatism.

Laws of Physics

An elephant tried to defy
Laws of physics, by learning to fly
She jumped from the bridge,
With the grace of a fridge,
Squashed a meerkat and two passers-by.

Modern Politics

Tooth Fairy accuses Santa of fraud.

Which Door?

Do you see the brilliance of the diamond,
    or notice the dust on the skirting board?

Do you hear the birds singing in the trees,
    or the harassed woman screaming at her kids?

Do you taste the rounded flavour of the wine,
    or the bitter tannins in the alcohol beneath?

Do you touch the ones you love, with tenderness,
    or hit out at those who hurt you?

Do you smell the fresh cut grass on a spring lawn,
    or the odour of dogs who have made their presence known?

Do you view the countryside in all its glory,
    or see the litter thrown thoughtlessly away?

Do you hear a choir of angels in the morning,
    or joints complaining as you cry yourself to sleep?

Do you taste the lightness of the pastry,
or does the sour taste of failure haunt your mouth?

Do you touch each moment with a thank you,
    or do you feel that hand of fickle fate?

Do you smell the flowers in your garden,
        or the scent of time that's passed you by?

Do you love life what'er the situation,
        or suffer life and take your medication?

Affects 1 in 100

Eye pain or rainbow vision!
Intermittent, blurring vision!
Yellow eyes or yellow skin!
Constipation! Vomiting!

Drowsiness and sleepiness!
Dizziness or shakiness!
Trouble with my flexion!
Problems with erection!
Weight loss! Weight gain!

Blocked nose and bladder pain!
Difficulties sleeping!
Changes in my speaking!
Hair loss! Milk loss!

Telling folk to get lost!
Tinnitus!
Convulsions!
Rashes or confusion!

Numbness! Tingling!
Fear of social mingling!
Sensitive to sunlight!
Wet bed! Is that right?

Such a wide variety
Has brought on my anxiety!

Prescribed me by my doc
These pills leave me in shock!

Once Upon a Time

There was a crook-ed man
And he ran a crook-ed house
And they all lived together
In America's White House.

Hide and Stink

Hide and seek, young Johnny had hidden
Up to his neck in a midden,
When they found him, he stunk
Much worse than a skunk
And to enter his house was forbidden.

Selfless?

Look at those fools, panic buying,
It's an absolute bloody disgrace,
Not like me, I'm not selfish,
Better double up though, just in case.

Boredom

Life in the lockdown
is boring.
Wouldn't it be good
to go out.

Dictionary pages
I'm reading.
Already I've learned
next to nowt.

Poetry Masterclass (by Dauphin the Dog)

I don't give a Nelly,
for a villanelle
or a bonnet,
for a fourteen-line sonnet.
I'd rather watch Bonanza
than struggle with a stanza.

A soliloquy
seems silly to me.
My nemesis
could be mimesis.
If I have a cold,
then I might say ode.
I'd never take a stance
on dissonance or assonance.

When I do meet up with Koo
I'll say howdy, not haiku.
I wouldn't give a meg
about a mixed up meter.
You can't lick a lyric
for good alliteration
and a well penned limerick,
can bring joy to a nation.

So, epic or ballad,
stick those syllabic rules.
Me and my mate Hobbo
are merely comic fools.

Ode to a Bogey

A wonderful thing is a bogey,
Ask any male child, if you've doubts.
He'll tell you, they're ever so tasty
and much better for you than sprouts.

Gerry Marsden, How Did You Do It?

His ferry has finally crossed,
His dreams are all tossed and blown,
Though the fans on the Kop may be lost,
Gerry, you will never walk alone.

Time Management

Stop rushing around!
You will end, in the ground.
Simply accept you are late
And don't get in a state.

The Race

Hare and tortoise
Had a race,
The tortoise came in
Second place.

And not because
His legs were teeny,
Hare was in
A Lamborghini.

Holes

A toilet roll
Without a hole,
Cylindrical
A useless whole.

A big Black Hole
Devoid of hole
Is big and black
But serves no role.

The footballer
Who scores a goal?
What use that goal
Without it's hole?

Spare a thought
For moles and voles
Where would they
be If they'd no holes?

Those bullets fired
Through rifled hole
Of killer's gun
On grassy knoll.

The men who dig
Holes in the street
Are proud of them
The street elite.

Our own bum-hole
Speaking of gas
Facilitates
Trapped wind to pass.

So now you know
That holes aren't zeros
Empty nothings…holes are heroes.

Black Clouds

Woke up.
Didn't want to.
In a foul mood.
Another resolution
Wasted.

Challenged God
to take me.
Didn't work.
Head thumping.
Stomach
gurgling,
Limbs trembling.

Feel awful.
Covid?
Don't think so.
More like
Death.

Drag myself up.
Walk-crawl to the bathroom.
Head bowed.
Let me die.
Please God!
I hate hangovers.

The Eve of What?

New Year's Eve is symbolic,
We should put on our glad rags and frolic
Though not anymore,
We were put in tier four,
So, pity the poor alcoholic.

New Covid Rules

Snow White
Is in Tier 4
And according
To the law,
Can only bubble
With one chappie
And he's a dwarf
But he is Happy!

A Chat with Dauphin the Dog

Hobbo: My Covid test has come back negative.
Dauphy: Oh dear!

Hobbo: Oh dear?
Dauphy: You told me to always be positive!

Hobbo: But a test should be negative.
Dauphy: So negative is positive?

Hobbo: It is.
Dauphy: Are you sure?

Hobbo: I'm positive!
Dauphy: Positive! You said you were negative.

Hobbo: I am.
Dauphy: You are what?

Hobbo: Negative.
Dauphy: And that's positive?

Hobbo: Yes.
Dauphy: Not negative?

Hobbo: No!
Dauphy: So, should I still be positive?

Hobbo: Yes.
Dauphy: But if I tested positive, that would be a negative?

Hobbo: It would.
Dauphy: So, I need to think positive, but be negative?

Hobbo: By Jingo, Dauphy, I think you've got it.
Dauphy: Who's Jingo?

Hobbo: Have you got it, Dauphy, or not?
Dauphy: I have. I have.

Hobbo: Positive?
Dauphy: Don't start.

The Meaning of Life

If the Hokey Cokey,
Is what it's all about,
Then throw me in the chokey,
And do not let me out!

Short-Lived Joy

Cruising for
A nice young man,
He found one,
Yin meets Yang.
Then his joy
Turned into panic
On board this ship,
They'd named Titanic.

Trouble Ahead

It cannot be done,
Said she
But he,
Out for fun,
Blew away all her doubts
And curried the sprouts.

A Lockdown Ditty

It's hard to be inspired
Whilst we're in lockdown mode,
I'm getting rather tired
Of treading that same road.

But when lockdown is over,
There'll be no stopping me,
Like a honeybee in clover,
I'll have so much to see.

The Pharmacy

Queued for an hour
Quite in distress,
Needing my tablets
To help me de-stress.

Along comes an addict,
For Methadone say,
Knocks at a side door
Is seen straight away.

Now if I were a chemist
Between me and you,
Other people come first
And the junkies could queue!

Socks

If socks
Are comfort food for feet,
Do clocks
Like seconds when they eat?

The Mighty Oak

Abandoned
by the squirrel,
the acorn
slowly awoke,
pushing tentative roots,
delicate as gossamer,
into the soft brown earth.

Toes
feeling their way,
inside a pair of fluffy slippers,
simultaneously
sending one tender shoot
upwards,
towards the warmth of the sun,
instinctively, timidly
not yet knowing
her destiny.

She swayed slightly
in the early Spring breeze,
looking up in astonishment
at the mighty oak
towering above her,
like a proud parent
and then…
she twigged.

Tha'll Need Some PPE
(To the tune of Ilkley Moor baht'at)

Tha's off to China for thee hols
Tha'll need some PPE
Tha's off to China for thee hols

Tha'll need some PPE
Tha'll need some PPE

Tha's gonna need some PPE
Tha'll need some PPE
Tha's gonna need some PPE

Tha'll need some PPE
Tha'll need some PPE
Tha'll need some PPE

Tha's gone and caught this dreaded bug
Tha'll need some PPE
Tha's gone and caught this dreaded bug

Tha'll need some PPE
Tha'll need some PPE
Tha'll need some PPE

So they've put thee in quarantine
Tha'll need some PPE
So they've put thee in quarantine

Tha'll need some PPE
Tha'll need some PPE
Tha'll need some PPE

We're all confined to tier three
Tha'll need some PPE
We're all confined to tier three

Tha'll need some PPE
Tha'll need some PPE
Tha'll need some PPE

But there's a vaccine on its way
Tha'll need some PPE
But there's a vaccine on its way

Tha'll need some PPE
Tha'll need some PPE
Tha'll need some PPE

Tha's forty one, tha's far too young
Tha'll still need PPE
Tha's forty one, Tha's far too young
Tha'll still need PPE
Tha'll still need PPE
Tha'll still need PPE

Tha'll: You will (pronounced tharl)
Tha's: You are (pronounced thars)
Thee: You

Dream Catcher

We live in a unique dream.
…and will wake up
on our glorious death.

Christmas 2020

It was Christmas Eve at Santa's
And Rudolph had not made the squad,
The others, were all out delivering
And he had been left on his tod.

A positive test had floored Rudolph
Suspected of Covid nineteen,
The North Pole was too isolated
To get there, with a virus vaccine.

The reindeer was sat with his feet up
Toasting his hooves by the fire,
His nose getting redder and redder,
The flames growing higher and higher.

Suddenly, whoosh, an explosion
Like the big bang, but more loud
Disturbed Rudolph's snooze by the fire,
Covering the world in a cloud.

His nose had ignited the fairy dust
Used to make presents for kids,
And the cloud which now covered our planet
Was it fatal? No, heaven forbids.

The dust was now targeting Covid
The virus was weakened, then killed
Now we all get to celebrate Christmas
And Rudolph, our hero, is thrilled.

The Owl and the Puddy Tat

The Owl and the Puddy Tat went to sea,
In Richard Branson's boat.
Their tax return Claims they both earn,
Much less than a five-pound note.

Noah's Muddy Ark

Noah was caught in the flood,
Up to his eyeballs in mud,
Needed a shove,
His wife says, my love,
The beasts, that you fleeced, are at stud.

Deaf, Me?

Your lunch is ready!
Freddie, who is Freddie?

It's lunch, it's on the table!
Mabel, when did you see Mabel?

Do you want to eat or not?
Ah, now you call me clot!

God, this is sooo frustrating!
Whaddya mean, I need castrating?

Put your flipping aids in!
You're rooting for a Saints win?

Where did I go wrong?
Can I sing a song?

Jeez, I've had enough!
I heard that, I'm not deaf!

You hear, when you've a hard on!
That's rude, I heard that, pardon?

The Learner

Penelope the porky pig,
For tasty truffles learned to dig.
The owner saw a little earner,
Though Penny dear, was but a learner.

Each one she found, she swiftly ate.
She ate the lot, and put on weight.
So, change of heart he sold her,
in yon restaurant, as filet mignon.

Be More Dog! by Dauphin

I don't ever fret about you
And there's no way I'd pick up your poo.
If I'm tired, then I drift off to sleep,
I have no need to work for my keep.

You feed me my meals twice a day,
When it's sunny, we go out to play,
I know you think this part's a pain,
But, I love our long walks in the rain.

I get muddy and dirty as hell
And I don't really care if I smell.
I love you with all my dog heart
When you fuss other dogs, do I start?

I'm the spit of a dog who just chills
Bit like you, when you've taken your pills
So relax man, this world ain't so crappy,
Be less man, be more dog, and be happy.

The Generation Gap

New hearing aids fitted today,
My grandson is very impressed,
They work on Bluetooth technology
Whatever that means, they're the best.

The Health Check

You need to cut down on the fags old man,
Forty a day is too many,
Reducing to twenty would be a good start,
Though really, you shouldn't have any.

I'll just check your blood pressure now,
if I may My, my, that's a hundred and forty!
If you weren't a key worker, I'd put you on sick,
Your whole way of life is so naughty.

You are heading towards diabetic,
With all those mince pies that you eat
And alcohol isn't a staple,
When you have it, it should be a treat.

I'll give you a jab for the virus,
But, be careful, should not go unsaid
And once your deliveries are finished,
I suggest that you go back to bed.

That's the end of your annual check-up,
I hope you pay heed to my banter
Your lifestyle must alter completely
Or next year, there won't be a Santa.

The Restaurant

"My sirloin is tough.
"...and this wine's a bit rough."

"It's busy, I know
"But service is slow."

"My soup's almost cold."

"This bread's five days old."

"Toilets are dirty."

"That waiter is shirty."

"Has B.O moreover."

"Shush, he's coming over."

"Ladies! Everything is fine?"

"Yes, thanks. Some more wine!"

Goosey Goose Gone

Her geese were a pair of old honkers,
That racket they made drove her bonkers.
The sound was a riot,
So, to get peace and quiet,
The male of the two lost his conkers.

A Good Night's Sleep

It slowly dawns on you
that you may have
drunk a smidgen too much
last night,
when you can't get comfortable
in bed and your wife wakes you,
to ask why
you are rolling around,
on the floor,
inside
the Ali Baba laundry basket.

The Baffled Blogger

There is no rhyme or reason,
To visitors and likes,
Though writing for a season,
I can't predict the spikes.

I work my socks off for a week
On something that goes flop,
Throw out nonsense, tongue in cheek
Which zooms straight to the top.

I thought I knew my audience,
Though clearly, I do not
It's either reader naughtiness
Or I have lost my plot.

Growing Old Gracefully

Two elderly men playing golf,
In the snow, in the midst of December
"Did you see where my tee shot went mate?"
"I did, but I cannot remember."

The Art of Biscuit Dunking

The biscuit was dunked in her tea,
Four seconds, not five and not three.
Her timing was wrong,
She held it too long
In it plopped, making cookie debris.

Perceptions

Drowning in a sea of
Despair, or floating on
An ocean of hope?

The Big Date

He splashed on the eau de cologne
For his date with this woman unknown,
It had no effect,
Despite their connect,
As the meeting was over the phone.

Behind the Mask

There's the kernel of a knuckle
Behind that ready chuckle,
The gaff that makes you laugh,
Which hides a paragraph
Of wit, incisive musing,
Disguised as light, amusing.
The poet tempting us to grin,
Achieves for both, result win-win.

But the bard that has me pause
And think about a cause,
The fist inside the glove,
The hawk behind the dove,
They sir have my blessing,
For 'tis more than window dressing.
This philosopher in rhyme,
A thinker, for our time.

The Daily Paradox

Undercover reporter,
sheds light
on conspirators,
conspiring against
conspiracy theories.

Dual Standards

A great tribal chieftain polygamous,
Met raven haired beauty monogamous,
He cherished his crown
But she wouldn't back down
So the kids that they had, stayed anonymous.

Bliss

The fleeting moment
Holding onto your dreams,
Before life revives you.

Sisters

One girl's hair is wavy,
Which fashion don't permit,
Hair straighteners, the answer,
They cost her quite a bit.

The sister's though is ramrod straight
But she wants wavy hair,
So she wraps it all in rollers,
Tell me, where's the logic there?

Happiness

Happiness,
a state of mind
depending
on nothing
but…
a state of mind.

Tiers (To Tears, a Song by the Late, Great Ken Dodd)

Tiers, for covid fears, are what you gave me,
Memories of a promise never kept,
You led me to believe lockdown's the answer
After all these lonely hours I've wept (with no one).

Tiers are my reward for isolation
But tiers can't mend my mental health, I must confess,
Let's forgive our peers uptown,
Turn our tiers of lockdown
Once more to tears of happiness.

Tiers are my reward for isolation
But tiers can't mend my mental health, I must confess,
Let's forgive our peers uptown,
Turn our tiers of lockdown
Once more to tears of happiness.

Let's forgive our peers uptown
Turn our tiers of lockdown
Once more to tears of happiness.

Mrs Hobbo

Hobbo: I'm in the bad books today, Dauphy.

Dauphy: Who with?

Hobbo: She who is never wrong.

Dauphy: Mrs Hobbo, what have you done this time?

Hobbo: I didn't do anything.

Dauphy: Something you said, again?

Hobbo: No, I didn't say anything.

Dauphy: So, it can't be the way that you said it this time?

Hobbo: No, it's what I was thinking.

Dauphy: Thinking!

Hobbo: That's what she said.

Dauphy: Dangerous territory, thought police!

Hobbo: I know, and the scary thing is, she was right.

Dauphy: Blimey.

Hobbo: I wish I was a dog sometimes.

Dauphy: Don't let Mrs Hobbo catch you thinking that, or you will be in trouble.

Hobbo: She already has!

The Church

First appearance,
One November,
Cried a bit
But don't remember.

Second time,
A lovely sight,
Never seen her
Dressed in white.

Last time there
The incense curled,
Couldn't smell it.
Dead to the world.

This Is the Baby

This is the baby, all alone
With a tenuous claim to the UK throne.

This is the royal, dubbed disloyal
Who fathered the baby, all alone
With a tenuous claim to the UK throne.

Here's the famous star, in a fancy car
Who married the royal, dubbed disloyal
Who fathered the baby, all alone
With a tenuous claim to the UK throne.

This is the chat, which caused a spat
With the famous star, in a fancy car
Who married the royal, dubbed disloyal
Who fathered the baby, all alone
With a tenuous claim to the UK throne.

These are the press, who made a mess
Reporting the chat, which caused a spat
With the famous star, in a fancy car
Who married the royal, dubbed disloyal
Who fathered the baby, all alone
With a tenuous link to the UK throne.

This is the news, that airs its views
About the press, who made a mess
Reporting the chat, which caused a spat
With the famous star, in a fancy car
Who married the royal, dubbed disloyal
Who fathered the baby, all alone
With a tenuous link to the UK throne.

This is the palace, that's been called callous
About the news, that airs its views
About the press, who made a mess
Reporting the chat, which caused a spat
With the famous star, in a fancy car
Who married the royal, dubbed disloyal
Who fathered the baby, all alone
With a tenuous claim to the UK throne.

This is the child, who is reconciled
With the palace, that's been called callous
About the news, that airs its views
About the press, who made a mess
Reporting the chat, which caused a spat
With the famous star, in a fancy car
Who married the royal, dubbed disloyal
Who fathered the baby, all alone
With a tenuous link to the UK throne.

Autumn

Autumn's reached, now we've retired,
Athletes shot, who've run their race.
No need for claims that we're inspired
At work, not told to watch our place.

For forty years we've done our share,
We put our shoulders to the plough,
No more mortgage, no more care,
It's time for some enjoyment now.

Kids are gone, we've scraped some savings,
We even get our pensions paid,
Shall we now indulge our cravings,
Spend this little pot we've made?

A cottage would be great, but face it,
We haven't got enough my dear.
A brand new car, so Scamp can chase it,
Frivolous, I hear you sneer.

We've talked at length, discussion's done,
Ambitious plans, and things beneath,
It's not a holiday in the sun,
It's hearing aids and brand new teeth.

My Body

I don't like my ears, I hate my nose
My weight, my face, my hair, my tum
My voice, my hands, my knees, my toes
But I do quite admire my bum.

Please

You say
That you love me
But you won't
Do that.
It's not a lot to ask.

Not all the time,
Just now and then
Would be nice,
To show that
You really do
Love me,
And it's not
Just words.

A little sign of respect
That would not
Go amiss,
I'm not asking a lot
Am I?

So please try it for once
It won't hurt you.
The next time
Perhaps,
I'd really appreciate it.

If
You could,
See your way to
Putting the seat down…

A Tough Life

The next time
You have the temerity
to complain
That your steak is tough,
Try to look at it
From the cow's perspective.

A Spectacle

Eyes, the window to our soul
But glasses let me see the hole
Into which I nearly fell,
Where's my specs, oh bloody hell!

Hurry Up!

Dinner's on the table,
Frustration in that shout,
Be down in just a minute
The turtle's head popped out.

The Gift

I bought my wife some bath bombs,
An anniversary gift,
Should have stuck to flowers,
She turned her nose up, sniffed.

She ran her bath that evening,
Romantically she sang.
As she shut the door behind her,
I waited for the bang.

Not a sausage, not a whimper,
They'd sold me bath bomb duds.
I'm going back tomorrow
For a refund on my goods.

Skin

I have just enough skin,
For the body I'm in.
How lucky is that?
Good job I'm not fat.
I would not have enough
To hide all my stuff,
You'd see my insides
And a lot more besides.

But if I'd just a touch,
Nay, a smidgen too much,
For the pounds that I weigh,
I'd look like a Shar Pei.
So here's to my skin
And the mish-mash within,
Epidermic, my treasure
Has been made to measure.

Generosity

Generosity
Towards our children, can be
Mistaken for wealth.

Votes

Trump and his admin divisive,
Though beaten by margins decisive
Claim Biden's a fraud
But the news from abroad,
Is the watching world think this derisive.

Friends

Simon was famous on Facebook,
Had hundreds of friends in his life,
Yet no one he actually spoke to,
No buddies, no girlfriend, no wife.

His success was repeated on Twitter
One million followers plus,
But he came to a violent ending,
Knocked down by the number nine bus.

The money he made from his adverts
Was left to his favourite quartet,
And mum organised a huge funeral
For all of his friends on the net.

Though no one showed up, not a sausage
To see Simon the Superstar off,
In reality, he was as popular
As a man with a bad Covid cough.

So, if you are an internet wizard,
With a wit that's as sharp as a knife,
Don't forget to engage with real people
Get up and get out, get a life.

Things That I Hate
(To Favourite Things by Rodgers and Hammerstein)

People who litter, and yobbos who spit,
Owners who thoughtlessly leave their dog's shit,
Wet windy weather and trains running late,
These are a few of the things that I hate.

The devious ways that the con man will scam,
Reality stars who do not give a damn,
Guys who know better but discriminate,
These are a few of the things that I hate.

Telephone calls where you don't get to speak,
Early hour visits to go for a leak
Food in the fridge that's beyond sell by date,
These are a few of the things that I hate.

When the sun shines,
When the birds sing,
When I'm feeling glad,
I simply remember the things that I hate,
And then I get really mad.
(Repeat)

The Wreck

Implants for mouth,
Aids to help hearing,
I feel like a car,
Relentlessly nearing

The end of its life,
Dear to maintain
Cost more and more
Money down drain.

Unlike the motor,
Can't trade me in,
Stuck with this body,
Pass me that gin.

Power

Top men thirst for power,
Politicians watch their back,
And women even claim
It's an aphrodisiac.

Yes, I admit I crave it,
Probably more than most,
If my leccy's cut again,
I'll have no beans on toast.

Hey Diddle Diddle

Hey diddle diddle,
My dad's on the fiddle
And mum's run away with a neighbour,
I'm in the pink
But I'm heading for clink,
Where my girlfriend, fifteen, is in labour.

Oh Heck!

Seems like a case of bad luck to me,
In agony, needs appendectomy
Flash of the blade,
Incision is made,
Surgeon thinks it's a vasectomy.

Planting Babies

When I questioned my mummy,
How I got in her tummy,
She said daddy had planted a seed.
Well that is a hard 'un,
Cos we have no garden,
And daddy does nothing but read.

A Four-Letter Word

This isn't a word
I use much in life
If I do, I'm in trouble
Most of all with my wife.

According to her
It's belittling and cheap
I admit, among men
We use it a heap.

It's a four letter word
That starts with a 'C'
Women don't like it
Demeans them you see.

The debate rages on
It is used all the time
But if I dare to say it
My life's not worth a dime.

So, you know how it starts
But those other three
I won't spell it out
But it ends with a 'T.'

And women don't like it
But men clearly do
For this four letter word
I have one final clue.

It is spoken the most
When out for a shop
Husbands open their mouths
And partners shout, "Stop."

Have you worked it out now
I know you're not lost
This troublesome word, well, it's quite simply…cost.

Loss

I lost my dear friend, Laura,
Won't ever see her again,
If I had gone before her,
She'd have caught the right damn train!

Bones

These bones of mine
Are bone idle.
They never move a muscle.

I get on fine
With nerves, I find
They are a real opuscule.

I could fall out,
Say bones, get out
Get veritably stroppy.

But I suppose
Without them bones,
I'd be a body floppy.

The Widow

When you promised,
Till death us do part
I never thought
It would happen.

Our Pet

wolf
lone, wild
hunting, preying, killing
woodsman, trapper, breeder, trainer
captures, selects, domesticates
faithful, loyal
companion.

Trust

Day that we met,
Best day of my life.

Day you broke my trust,
Cried myself to sleep.

Day you came back,
I couldn't be arsed.

Lunch

The flames were prolific,
The heat was terrific,
The words from the kitchen profane,
My nice chicken roast,
Is burned black as toast,
Sunday lunch has been ruined again.

Little Old Beer Drinker
(To Little Old Wine Drinker, by Dean Martin)

I'm praying for rain in sunny Shropshire,
So the hops can swell and they can brew more beer,
And I'm standing in a chippy here in Bradford,
With a thumping head and a ringing in my ear.

I ask the man behind the counter for an aspirin,
And he answers as he serves me pie and peas,
This is a chip shop not a bloody chemist,
I say, "Little ol' beer drinker me."

I came here last week from up in Grimsby
Cos my baby left for Clacton by the sea,
When they ask, "Who's the man who's got a cob on?"
I say, "Little ol' beer drinker me."

I ask the man behind the counter for an aspirin,
And he answers as he serves me pie and peas,
"This is a chip shop, not a bloody chemist,"
I say, "Little ol' beer drinker me."
I say, "Little ol' beer drinker me."
Little ol' beer drinker me.

A Poem About Anything

Anything can make us cry,
Anything will make us sing,
Anything may cause a sigh
Anything, make you a king.

Anything is big or small,
Anything could be something
Anything is nought at all,
Anything, a mere nothing.

Anything, we writers write
I give my all for anything,
Anything, both day and night,
Anything is everything.

The Medical

There's snow on the hills
And I've taken my pills.
The psychiatrist thinks me quite sane.
The pigs in the sky,
Yes I know they can't fly,
But they're taking a test just the same.

The voice in my head
That is never quite dead,
Is singing a sad kind of ditty.
I try to write songs
Yet they come out all wrong,
All clangers and smash, more's the pity.

I've got an IQ
Of a hundred and two,
Which puts me ahead of a half-wit.
I'm friends with the Queen
And my washing machine,
But give me a dollar, I'd halve it.

I live on the moon
With an ageing baboon
Who is wanted in five different countries?
My favourite meal
Is strawberry peel
Which I harvest each autumn from plum trees.
The doc's here again.
She insists, I am sane.

She has the last laugh, no disputing.
The stupid old lush,
I'm as daft as a brush.
Speak to my grandma, Rasputin.

Tick-Tock, round the clock,
I need a new frock.
Tear drop, splobalop, I am barmy.
Boogaloo bongos,
Dingos and drongos,
I don't want to play in your army.

Democracy

More dead from Covid nineteen
Then were killed in fourteen-eighteen,
Second World War, Vietnam
And still this man doesn't give a damn.

Democracy, well that's a joke,
The wishes of ordinary folk
Discounted on merely a whim,
But not if you voted for him.

Girl Power

Remember, remember, the fifth of November,
The UK's in lock-down again
To beat this disease, sack all the MP's,
Put a woman in charge, with a brain.

Steam

Warm shower, cold bathroom, steam,
Warm wife, cold husband
Probably divorce.

Gran's Clock

Hickory Dickory Dock
My gran left me a clock,
Chimed all blooming night
So, come the daylight,
I threw the damn thing in the loch.

House to Home

house
empty, unloved
valued, marketed, sold
parents, children, friends, family
inhabited, fixed, transformed
treasured, happy
home.

Grooming

I snipped a hair from out my ear,
A full three inches long,
From where on earth did that appear?
I'm getting like King Kong.

Best Holiday Ever

We should never have chosen off peak,
It was raining, the car sprang a leak,
David squashed granny's best hat,
Baby Alfie was sick on the cat.

On the moors, dad ran over a ram,
An hour later, we're stuck in a jam.
We got there too late for the ferry,
Mum found the bar and got merry.

We arrived there to find we'd left gran,
At the caff, with a man from Japan.
Our five star was under construct
And all of the rooms double-booked.

The bathroom and toilet were dirty,
The waiters and waitresses shirty,
My purse and my handbag got nicked
And our sightseeing coaches were bricked.

The food gave young Lucy the trots
And Christopher broke out in spots,
German measles, our French doctor said
And confined him to ten days in bed.

Paragliding, my mum sprained her back,
Sadly, dad had a mild heart attack.
We learned from a broker named Khalid
Our insurance was no longer valid.

Going home, despite begging and pleading,
Dad got a ticket for speeding.
When the copper told dad he could start,
Our tyres were as flat as a fart.

Once home, track-traced for Covid 19,
So then, yes you've guessed, quarantine
And because we are now isolating,
This vacation gets zero star rating.

My Engine

When I was younger
I'd go for a spin.
So great was my hunger,
I'd drive to Berlin.

As I got older,
Hand on my heart,
The engine was colder,
I'd need a bump start.

The motor's got mucky,
First starts, then it stops.
Some days I'd be lucky
To get to the shops.

Now, seized and rusty,
Where once it all shone,
My tried and my trusty
Has got up and gone.

Equality

The king is dead, long live the king,
So those heraldic angels sing.
Here lies he, in princely state,
Mortal man, to whom his fate,
Death that leveller of us all,
Cares not for goods, for wherewithal.

No difference makes, for rank, or status.
Keeps for each, this forced hiatus.
What use now those jewels, that wealth?
Lost is that youth, that life, that health.
Our time is precious, borrowed must
Be handed over. We, to dust.

Books

A book fell on my head,
Yes, landed on myself,
I know that I'm well read,
But I have to blame my shelf.

Curry

The bottom fell out of my world
When you left me gutted and rotten,
So, I went on my own for a curry
Then the world fell out of my bottom.

Chillin'

Whilst watching I.P.L
I had an I.P.A,
The cricket rather swell
The beer was way okay.

I.P.L Indian Premier League cricket
I.P.A India Pale Ale beer.

The Gigolo

The gigolo didn't have much
In his trousers, specifically crutch,
When the ladies got rude
He said, "I am no prude.
You can look, but you'd better not touch."

The Victory

Oh, how we long for the buzz of a crowd,
The hustle and bustle, the shouting out loud.
United, one voice, a community choir
Inciting, exciting as voices get higher.
Fiercely protective, allegiances proud,
As pent up frustrations are vented aloud.

The shame of the game, when our team goes one down
A penalty! Referee! That man is a clown.
The waster finds space to, nip through, equalise
Stick that up your kilt, and try that on for size.
Two more, take what for, now our world's upside down
Subdued is the mood, in the wrong half of town.

So, it's off to the pub with the rest of the crew.
The reds, put to bed, and the team are all blue.
Ecstatic, emphatic, a victory, a win
Can't wait for the date when we do it again.
Our hopes for the cup are rekindled anew,
Forgetting last week, we were thankful they drew.

Amazing Facts

It's true, if you tickle a rat
It laughs, well how about that?
And a butterfly taste with its feet
Come on, admit it, that's neat.

Another fact, prick up your ears
Snails sleep for up to three years
But this one is way off the charts
Octopuses, they have three hearts!

Vandalism

Grave vandalised,
Surprise, surprise
Of Cilla OBE.
Though not a saint,
Why spray with paint,
It seems bizarre to me.

Doddy too,
What Diddy do?
He brought us happiness.
Both rest in peace,
It's just caprice,
Some folks are bad, I guess.

Vacation

They've found water on the moon,
Might be enough to drink,
This news could not have come too soon,
For holidays, I think.

No need for social distancing,
No more Covid 19,
I feel so happy, I could sing,
Somewhere I haven't been.

I'll take a bucket and a spade,
My pint glass for the pub,
A brolly too for in the shade,
I hope they serve good grub.

I'm all packed up and set to go,
Need Boris's decree,
Because the little so and so
Has put me in tier three.

The Flu Jab

Oh, it's good to be alive,
I'm really quite excited,
At the tender age of sixty-five.
For my flu jab, I'm invited.

The nurse (Fat and gum-chewing)
Drew a target on my bum,
Asked, "What do you think you're doing?"
Replied, "It's social distance chum."

My trembling arm she grabbed
And joked, "Don't worry matey,
The last one that I stabbed,
I scored the max, one eighty."

So, now I'm flu resistant,
I should be feeling cool
But, Covid's more persistent
And I'm nobody's fool.

Question Time

Question time,
With P.M. Boris,
Get more sense
From great aunt Doris.

Opposition though,
Keir Starmer,
Charisma of
A Yorkshire farmer.

Just Eat

In his wishes, Vinny's missus
Let him play out, catching fishes.
Not for him the cluck it, pluck it,
Finger lickin' bargain bucket.
While he's on the River Ouse
His missus rings Deliveroo's.
Checks out Chinese for her daughter
Orders more than what she oughta.

Fish and chips, tortilla teasers,
Salad dips and spicy pizzas.
Vinny's mini's home for supper
Annie's plans he tries to scupper.
Not for him the angler's boasting
All he wants is cheesy toasties.
Wherein she turns, and out she swishes
And Vin, he learns, to do the dishes.

First Encounter

I spied her in the cafe,
Dipping brioche, chocolate chipped,
She said she was Parisian,
"Why, that's capital," I quipped.

Old Friends

There are holes in my sock
And a hole in my shoe,
They have been round the block
And my toes all peek through.

I could buy some more
But I've got quite attached,
They were worn to the funeral
When my wife was dispatched.

Children

Children talk of
Monsters and Santa,
Adults engage in
Cruel banter.

Kids believe
In the Easter bunny,
Grown-ups worship
The power of money.

Children want
Sweets, hugs and toys,
Adults seek
Refuge from noise.

Anything naughty
An adult forbids,
What adults want mostly,
They want to be kids.

Tattoos

I've thought about one
But I'm scared of the pain,
Will it fade with the sun
Or wash off with the rain?

A small one to start,
Nothing too flash,
Perhaps a love-heart.
Do I have to pay cash?

The tattooist's gun
Starts up with a whine,
My idea of fun?
Nope, I've changed my mind.

Polly

Polly put the kettle on,
What a clever bird.
Bought online from Amazon,
Obeys my every word.

The Canine Poet by Dauphin

I tried to draft a careful poem
Of length, with strength, a testing tome.
The final draft though, monochrome,
It should have stayed in house, at home.

So, I turned to trite, a ditty,
Should have learned, as far from pretty.
Try to force iambic meter,
Like compulsive overeater.

Talent turns to trad. a sonnet,
Boy, that's just as bad, it's chronic.
This queer compulsion to get rhyme
To scan, oh man, it's such a crime.

I'll try some prose, see how that goes,
A budding Rowling, no one knows.
That's it, my friend, I'll write a book
With twisted end to get you hooked.

Pen a song, with awesome lyrics,
Dance floor flooded atmospherics.
Writing now, on upward spiral,
Fame and fortune, even viral.

Name in lights, and big star billing.
Upbeat dog treats, snoozing, chilling.
Win awards, a prize, a trophy,
Accolades and "Well done, Dauphy."

Predictive Text

I wrong this poet on me phone
With the aim of predictable sex,
It worms in ounce by itself
Knots who to tyre next.

Choice

My wife has bought me two ties
As part of my birthday surprise,
I wore one tonight
"Is the other not, right?"
She criticised, rolling her eyes.

Pandemic

Is a pandemic
Systemic
Of too many
Pans
On the planet?
It can't
Mean that,
Can it?

Vanishing Youth

You are no longer in your youth,
So I'll remove that pesky tooth.
I know there's wisdom in it
But we're going to have to bin it.

Brace yourself for this injection,
I'll get rid of your nasty infection
And the toothache that was raging
Is now a gap, first sign of ageing.

Your mouth will start to droop
But you can have a little soup
Now, if you're feeling better,
Here's my bill and Thank You letter.

Books

Unbelievable,
Horror, sci-fi, fiction.
You couldn't make it up.

Compromise

Wife Calm, unhurried.
Shopping, browsing, choosing.
Car, newspaper, crossword, sweets
Reading, chewing, waiting
Impatient, moody
Husband.

Paper

The world is using less paper,
Most of my books are on Kindle.
This must be a good thing, right?
As all of our rain-forests dwindle.

I don't even use any cash now,
I pay everything credit card
But how do I wipe my bum though?
This laptop's too rigid, too hard.

I Wandered Lonely

I wandered lonely as a tramp,
A president, or five times champ.
In splendid isolation, I
Could see with my objective eye,
How all life's problems spring from men
Who, power crave, like oxygen.
See in terms of nihilistic,
No time for the altruistic.

Who think the world a giant gem,
To plunder, pillage, all for them.
What use they, the artist, poet
Sentiment, they durst not show it.
What excuse, tyrant, dictator
When you come to meet your maker?
Sowing bitter seeds of hatred
Were your passions ever sated?

Money is the root of evil,
Love will triumph, always, we will
Strive to help out one another,
Mother, father, sister, brother
So that in that final reckoning
We will find our loved ones beckoning.

Emancipation

The plane at the end of the runway
Ground to a halt, engine stalled.
It's captain, to fix it, knew one way
And for a mechanic she called.

The lady came out with her hammer,
Soon had it fixed, with no sweat.
A motorised sort of a stammer,
Technically called Stutterer Jet.

Owl

The commonest bird in Great Britain
Not sea bird, not game bird, not fowl
This bird's to be found in your kitchen
It's everyday name, the Teat Owl.

If Schools

If wheels were square
Instead of round,
Cars would be useless
For getting around.

If schools were round
Instead of square,
There'd be no naughty corner
And no naughty chair.

Poet's Inheritance

I have realised, when I cark it,
What will become of my blog?
Who can I trust with my laptop,
My buddy, my missus, my dog?

So, I'm now looking for an apprentice,
To train 'ere I finally go
Otherwise, you will wake up one morning,
To no more little

Images

In the natural world, the male
Is often full of colour,
Whilst the female can be dull,
Her backside, a little fuller.

In the human world, a male
May sport a big fat belly,
From drinking too much beer
And watching too much telly.

Springtime

Woody fingers silhouetted,
Spring sap rising warm, has wetted
Buds which break out in the sunlight,
Leaves unfurl before the bun-fight.
Birds find voices, sing in choirs
Courting couple, stops, admires.

Cherry blossom, pink confetti,
Winter blues, forgotten, petty.
Springtime bloom, a time for giving,
Breathes fresh life in all things living.
A chance to start afresh, renew
So where'd I put that barbecue?

Ponder

I pondered the meaning of life
Gave it some serious thought,
The answer, the edge of a knife
Either beer, or then again, sport.

Granddad

Granddad loved his dogs,
He'd kept them all his life
So, when he popped his clogs
He left one to his wife.

Politicians

Bill and Ben, the flowerpot men
Talked rubbish, splobalop,
When politicians do it then,
Is it something they can't stop?

Fish and Chips

Fish chips and mushy peas,
sorted out my life,
like you would not believe.

Johnny

Little Johnny, he needed to go
But teacher refused, she said, "No,
What word starts with a P?"
He said, "You're asking me,
Really Miss, you're the one who should know."

Dear Diary

Monday dentist, Tuesday doctor's,
(Socially apart),
Wednesday have my hearing checked,
Thursday, specialist for my heart.

Friday, get my toupee cleaned,
Saturday, food from shops,
Sunday, Covid lockdown
And all my pleasure stops.

The Trip

"You've been a really good boy,
So here is what we'll do,
You can have a brand new toy
Or, I'll take you to the zoo."

Johnny paused his keypad,
Used to being admonished,
This offer from his dad,
Had left him quite astonished.

To Chester Zoo they travelled,
Dad talked of birds and bees
Which left young Johnny baffled,
"Can you explain it, daddy please?"

"Watch the animals, son,
And the little things they do,
When they are having fun,
We humans do that too."

The young boy watched with care,
He was always wide awake,
The monkeys and a bear,
A crocodile, a snake.

Creatures that were hairy,
Some which made him laugh,
The tigers, they were scary
And he loved the tall giraffe.

When the day was almost finished,
Johnny knew what grown-ups do,
"Don't look much fun to me, dad,
Do I have to eat my poo?"

The Face

This wrinkled old face
in the shaving mirror,
reflecting my whole life.

Mates

Two real good mates
Meet up in a pub,
They have a great time
And eat lots of grub.

They drink loads of beer
Then, needing a wee,
They follow each other
It's normal, you see.

One says to the other
"This trough's a bit high."
"Mine's longer," says he
"I'll give it a try."

Then he looks across,
A girl's washing her hands
It's a sink, not a trough,
Smart, he understands.

They've gone in the ladies,
Instead of the gents
The lass does not laugh,
Pays no compliments.

Both so embarrassed
The two stop mid-pee,
Then zip up their trousers
And giggling, they flee.

Alcohol and Me

Alcohol and me,
Now that's a complex one,
Makes me do some stupid things
But I've had a lot of fun.
The life and soul of parties,
Singing karaoke,
Remembering all the gags
That's me, Mr Jokey.

I've got myself in states,
Nowhere near my best,
I've been sick on the streets,
And woken fully dressed.
Things I am ashamed of,
Which sober, wouldn't do
But drink gave me the courage
To whisper, "I love you."

And you are everything
So tell me, in the end,
Is drink one of my demons
Or a very fickle friend?

Eternity

Eternal dark, eternal light,
No one can be certain,
If our eternal soul takes flight
When life closes its curtain.

Canine Therapy

If your world's in a mess
And your mind's in a fog,
If you're feeling depressed,
Grab a leash, walk the dog.

If your love life is crap
And you need a good snog,
If your boyfriend's got clap,
Grab a leash, walk the dog.

If you can't find your prince,
And you're stuck with a frog,
If you've lost your blue rinse,
Grab a leash, walk the dog.

If you're fed up at home,
Sick of cleaning the bog,
You've no teeth in your comb,
Grab a leash, walk the dog.

If you want high heeled shoes,
And you've only one clog,
When you've got Monday blues,
Grab a leash, walk the dog.

You are driving the motor,
But you're just a small cog,
Then, stuff that new rota,
Grab a leash, walk the dog.

If you married a hunk,
And he turned out, a hog
There's no need to get drunk,
Grab a leash, walk the dog.

If your drink is cocktail,
And you're given eggnog,
Put some wind in your sail,
Grab a leash, walk the dog.

So, when nothing seems right
In your back catalogue,
Make the world look brighter,
Grab a leash, walk the dog.

Loyalty

Grocer Jack,
In cul-de-sac,
Head full of smack,
Tripped on a crack,
On his way back
From the 'Duck with no Quack'.

This maniac,
Was taken aback,
Fell with a whack,
Causing crise cardiaque.
Revived with a snack
And a double cognac,
From a girl in a sack,
With a dad called Jack.

The Bookworm

I scored three goals in sports today.
Hat trick hero? Hmm. No way!
Playing what I think is flanker,
Earned the nickname own-goal wanker.

Leaves

If leaves fell up
Instead of down,
When they turn yellow
Then go brown.
The sky would soon
Be overcrowded
And leave our sun
Forever shrouded.
Gravity though,
Serves to attract,
So things fall down
And that's a fact.

Deafness

Invisible problem,
socially excluded,
deaf as a fish.

Cricket

Sprawled on the couch, watching the cricket
My team went and lost their last wicket
"Cheer up my dear,
I've brought you a beer."
"Why, thank you, love. That's just the ticket."

A Nod to Mr Lear

Limericks, are meant to be funny,
Not taken too seriously, honey.
I did what you said,
When you took me to bed?
So, shut up and give me the money.

Yorkshire-Born Rhapsody
(To Bohemian Rhapsody by Freddie Mercury)

I've had a real life,
Not tried no Ecstasy,
Stuck to the Tetley's,
My escape from reality.
Tell you no lies
Look back on my life and see,
Council estate boy, I got no sympathy
Because my friends would come, friends would go
Bullied high, bullied low,
Anyway, I must grow, teachers turned a blind eye
To me, to me.

Mama, she tried her best,
Escaped whilst I still could,
Got a woman, did me good
Mama, I invented love
But now old age just took it all away.
Mama, aahhh,
It sure makes me want to cry
The things I've lost, I won't get back tomorrow,
It's all gone, it's all gone
Like the rain that pitter patters.

Too late, the way we were,
Young people loads of time,
Bodies searching perfect rhyme

Two a.m. everybody, I've got to go,
Gotta get up from my bed and take a pee
Mama, aahhh (any way the splash flows),
I don't want to age,
I sometimes wish I'd never done anything dumb.

I see a little nervous shadow of myself,
Too much beer, too much wine, banging all night on the banjo,
Boddingtons and curry, always in a hurry, me.
Way we were oh, way we were oh
Way we were oh, way we were oh
Way we were has got to go, oh no, oh no.

I'm just an old man, and nobody sees me
He's just an old man, last in the family,
His Alzheimer's could be senility.

Youth'll cry, youth'll sigh, let the old man die,
No way mate! No, we will not let him die. Let him die
No way mate. We will not let you die. Let him die
No way mate! We will not let him die. Let him die
Will not let him die. Let him die (never)
Never, never, never, never, never let him die,
Why, why, why, why, why, why, why
Oh God in heaven, God in heaven, God in heaven let me die,
In Wetherspoons has the barmaid raised a glass
To me
To me

So you think you will not lose that glint in your eye,
So you think you can stay young and you'll never die,
Oh baby, it's impossible baby
You're gonna grow old, you're gonna grow old before long
Ahh yeah, aahhh yeah.

Does life really matter?
Are we all born free,
Does life really matter?
Yes, life really matters to me.

Anyway the mind goes…

Beefy

What an amazing award
They made Ian Botham a Lord
The Queen said, "Arise."
Then to Beefy's surprise
She hit him for six with her sword.

The Park Bench

I could tell you some tales
About bums on this bench.
There's that woman from Wales,
A fine, sturdy wench.

The elderly couple
Who stop for a brew.
She's not so supple,
And he's eighty-two.

The kids who pop by
To play hide and seek,
Or in winter, I Spy,
Is it bird? Is it beak?

But of all those I ease,
My favourite pair,
Is the courting strip-tease
With their legs in the air.

Old Age Pensioner

Today, I get O.A.P status
A tribute to my apparatus.
It's downhill from here,
After sixty-six years,
My hernia is on a hiatus.

Shorts

Downtown in Burnley the people wear shorts,
Perhaps it's a Lancashire thing,
Baring knees at the first sign of Summer
And airing them, through until Spring.

Calves that are shapely, knees that are knobbly,
Legs that could win the Gold Cup,
Braving arctic conditions, blowing a hooley,
These things should be kept covered up.

In cold or in rain, folk put on their coats
Whilst waiting for sunnier skies,
But even in wellies, they're still wearing shorts,
Must be something they put in their pies.

Insomnia

House is asleep
Apart from me,
I've counted sheep,
I went for a pee.

Sheets in a heap,
Partner snoring,
She is in deep,
God this is boring.

It's just turned three,
Street's so quiet,
I'll make some tea
And sod the diet.

Tea did not work,
Gave me heartburn,
Feel such a berk,
Will I never learn?

Read till I ache,
Just start to drift,
Shaken awake,
"You're on early shift."

Covid

Often a target for bullies,
Not the handsomest kid in the shop
But over the last month or so,
The teasing has come to a stop.

Now, I can join in with the others.
"Why's that?" you might very well ask,
Well, it's thanks to the outbreak of Covid
You see, I look great in a mask.

Black Lives Matter

Black people, equal…
One small step for man
A giant leap for mankind!

Ingram Content Group UK Ltd.
Milton Keynes UK
UKHW021827260423
420831UK00003B/25